MW00851051

# Joseph Haydn
# STRING QUARTETS
## Opp. 42, 50 and 54

Edited by Wilhelm Altmann

DOVER PUBLICATIONS, INC.
NEW YORK

This Dover edition, first published in 1982, is an unabridged republication of ten separate quartet volumes (Op. 42; Op. 50, Nos. 1–6; and Op. 54, Nos. 1–3) as published by Ernst Eulenburg Ltd., London (n.d.; publication numbers 154, 167, 168, 169, 112, 155, 156, 54, 66 and 113, respectively, of the Edition Eulenburg, or Eulenburg Miniature Scores).

Manufactured in the United States of America
Dover Publications, Inc.
180 Varick Street
New York, N.Y. 10014

Library of Congress Cataloging in Publication Data

Haydn, Joseph, 1732-1809.
    [Quartets, strings. Selections]
    String quartets opp. 42, 50, and 54.

    Reprint. Originally published: London : Eulenburg.
    1. String quartets—Scores. I. Altmann, Wilhelm, 1862-1951. II. Haydn, Joseph, 1732-1809. Quartets, strings, H. III, 43, D minor. 1982. III. Haydn, Joseph, 1732-1809. Quartets, strings, H. III, 44-49. 1982. IV. Haydn, Joseph, 1732-1809. Quartets, strings, H. III, 57-59. 1982.
M452.H42A4   1982                           81-15311
ISBN 0-486-24262-5                          AACR2

785.7471
H415s

# CONTENTS

# Op. 42, in D Minor

## I

# II

**Menuetto**
**Allegretto**

Trio

Menuetto D. C.

# III

Adagio e cantabile

# IV

# Op. 50, No. 1, in B-flat Major

## I

# II

**Adagio non lento**

# III

**Poco Allegretto**

Trio

D.C. al Fine

# IV

**Finale**
**Vivace**

# Op. 50, No. 2, in C Major

I

Joseph Haydn, Op. 50, No 2
1732-1809

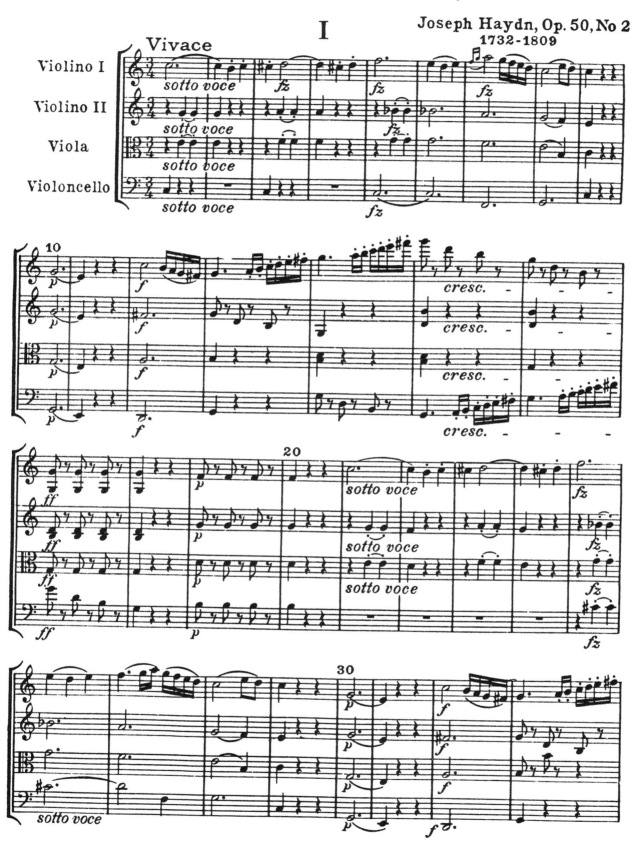

# II

**Adagio. Cantabile**

# III

**Menuetto. Allegretto**

Menuetto D.C.

# IV

**Finale. Vivace assai**

# Op. 50, No. 3, in E-flat Major

## I

II

Andante più tosto Allegretto

Trio

60

70

80

Menuetto D.C.
al Fine

# IV

**Finale Presto**

# Op. 50, No. 4, in F-sharp Minor

## I.

# II.

III.

Menuetto. Poco Allegretto

Menuetto D.C.

# IV.

**Finale Fuga**
**Allegro moderato**

# Op. 50, No.5, in F Major

## I

# II

Poco Adagio

# III.

**Menuetto Allegretto** ♩. = 63

Menuetto D.C.

# IV

**Finale.** Vivace

# Op. 50, No. 6, in D Major

## I.

# II.

Poco Adagio

# III.

**Menuetto Allegretto**

# IV.

Finale  Allegro con spirito

# Op. 54, No. 1, in G Major

## I

**II**

Allegretto

## III

Menuetto
Allegretto

# Op. 54, No. 2, in C Major

## I

# II

# III

**Menuetto**
**Allegretto**

# IV

Finale
Adagio

# Op. 54, No. 3, in E Major

## I

Allegro

Joseph Haydn, Op. 54  N?3
1732-1809

# II

Largo cantabile

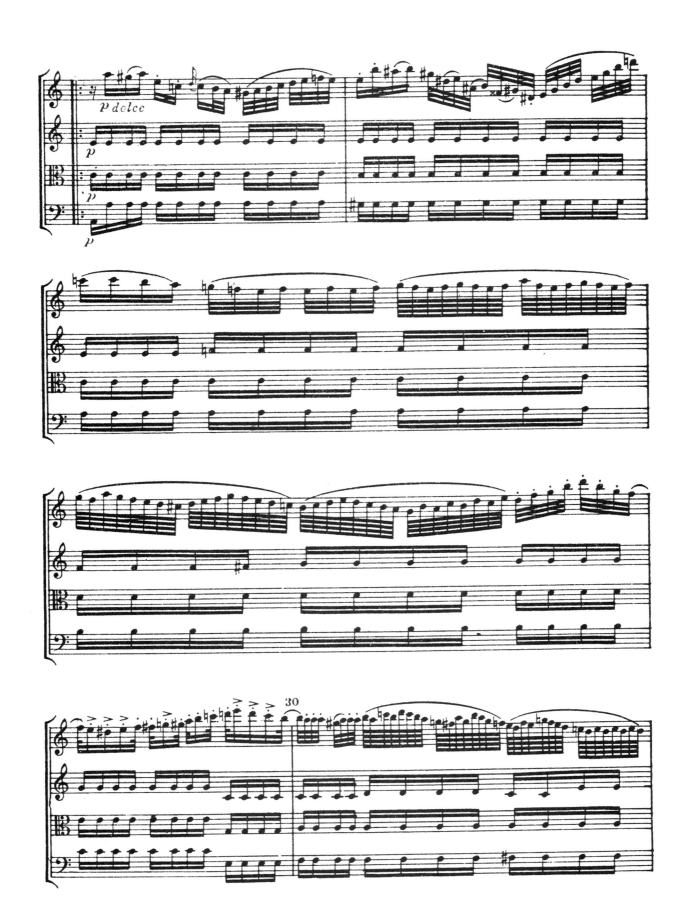

**III**

Menuetto
Allegretto

Trio

40

50

M. D. C.

# IV

Finale
Presto